My First OXFORD Book of Words

Illustrated by David Melling
Compiled by Neil Morris

OXFORD
UNIVERSITY PRESS

For Bosiljka, Branko and Igor Sunajko.

D.M.

OXFORD
UNIVERSITY PRESS

Great Clarendon Street, Oxford OX2 6DP

Oxford New York
Athens Auckland Bangkok Bogotá Buenos Aires Calcutta
Cape Town Chennai Dar es Salaam Delhi Florence Hong Kong Istanbul
Karachi Kuala Lumpur Madrid Melbourne Mexico City Mumbai
Nairobi Paris São Paulo Singapore Taipei Tokyo Toronto Warsaw
and associated companies in Berlin Ibadan

Oxford is a registered trade mark of Oxford University Press

Illustrations copyright © David Melling 1999
Text copyright © Oxford University Press 1999

First published 1999

1 3 5 7 9 10 8 6 4 2

British Library Cataloguing in Publication Data
Data available

ISBN 0–19–910419–0

Printed in Italy

Contents

Look at Me!   4-5
Our House   6-7
Off to School   8-9
Our Classroom   10-11
Colour Fun   12-13
When I Grow Up   14-15
Long Time Ago   16-17

Busy Shopping   18-19
Monster Lunch   20-21
Time to Play   22-23
On the Farm   24-25
At the Beach   26-27

Birthday Party   28-29
Animal Magic   30-31
In the Bath   32-33
Time for Bed   34-35

My ABC   36-37
Count 123   38-39
Shapes   40-41
Opposites   42-43
Weather   44
Time   45

Index   46-47

Look at Me!

chest

leg

foot

toe

back

elbow

bottom

finger

tummy

knee

hand

hair

arm

head

shoulders

4

face

cheek

ear

eye

chin

mouth

teeth

tongue

neck

nose

girl

boy

5

Our House

roof

dustbin

gate

stairs

chimney

fence

garage

window

door

dog cat

rabbit

spider snail

letters

post bag

leaf flower

tree

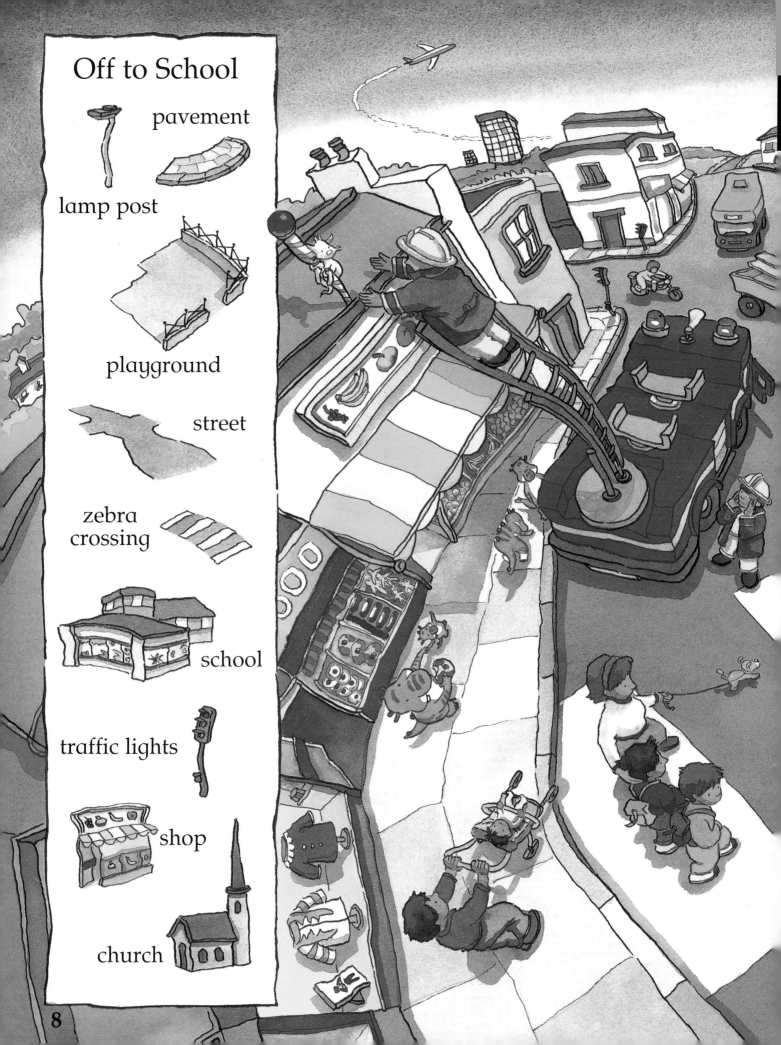

Off to School

pavement

lamp post

playground

street

zebra crossing

school

traffic lights

shop

church

8

bicycle

car

bus

motorbike

fire engine

truck

helicopter

ambulance

plane

9

Our Classroom

school bag

book

lunch box

blackboard

chalk

globe

desk

magnet

bin

10

cassette recorder

cassette

ruler

computer

map

disk

dice

keyboard

mouse

11

Colour Fun

black

blue

brown

green

grey

orange

pink

purple

red

white

yellow

12

overalls

glue

painting

paintbrush

paints

pencil

paper

scissors

felt pen

easel

13

When I Grow Up

postman

builder

doctor

police officer

vet

footballer

firefighter

bus driver

14

train driver

pop star

pilot

dancer

diver

cook

astronaut

lifeguard

15

Long Time Ago

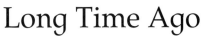

Dinosaurs:
200 million years ago

Tyrannosaurus Rex

Stegosaurus

Diplodocus

Triceratops skeleton

fossil

bone

Busy Shopping

trolley

basket

cash register

bread

bun

jam

cereal

potatoes

sausages

spaghetti

milk

yoghurt

cheese

eggs

apple

banana

orange

tomato

carrot

lettuce

19

Monster Lunch

cooker

fridge

washing machine

saucepan

iron

cup

bowl

knife

fork

kettle

plate

spoon

saucer

chair

teapot

cushion

sofa

stereo

table

television

video recorder

vacuum cleaner

Time to Play

doll's house

doll

game

racing car

robot

jigsaw puzzle

teddy

train set

22

drum

guitar

keyboard

microphone

trumpet

recorder

cymbals

bells

tambourine

23

On the Farm

horse

chicken

cock

duck

goose

sheep

goat

pig

cow

24

tractor

stream

bridge

field

forest

hay

hill

scarecrow

At the Beach

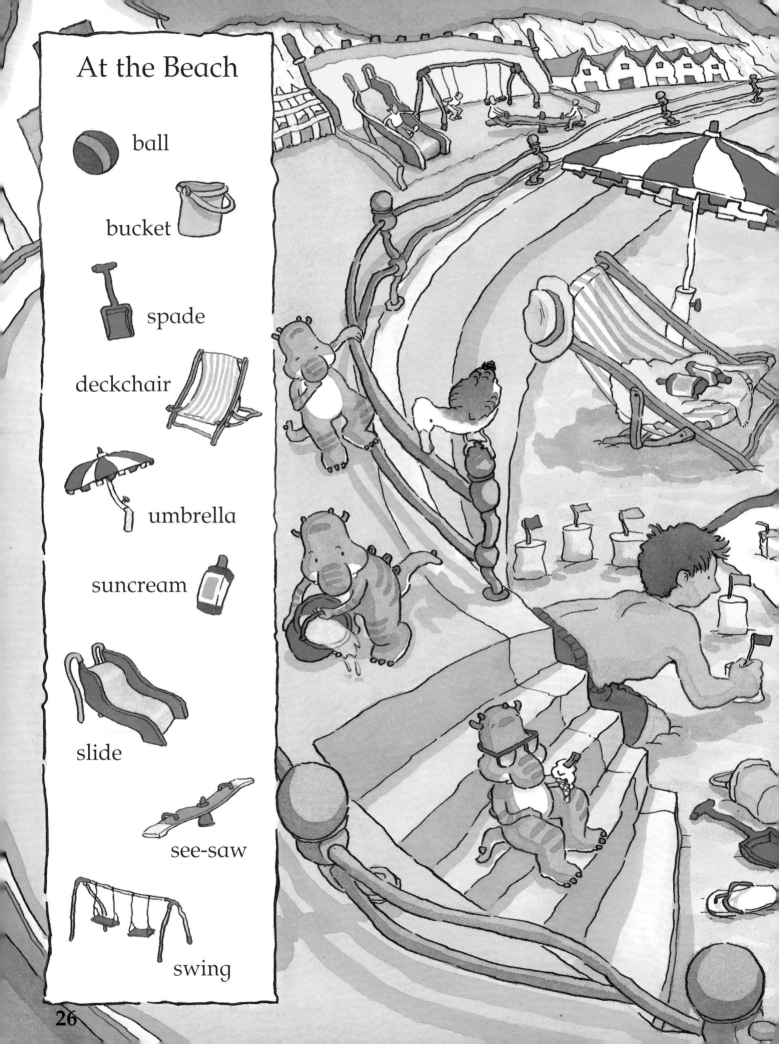

ball

bucket

spade

deckchair

umbrella

suncream

slide

see-saw

swing

ship

lighthouse

sandcastle

seagull

shell

crab

octopus

starfish

seaweed

Birthday Party

birthday card

candle

balloon

present

streamer

party blower

party hat

wand

magician

sweets

sandwich

pizza

ice cream

chocolate

biscuit

straw

drink

cake

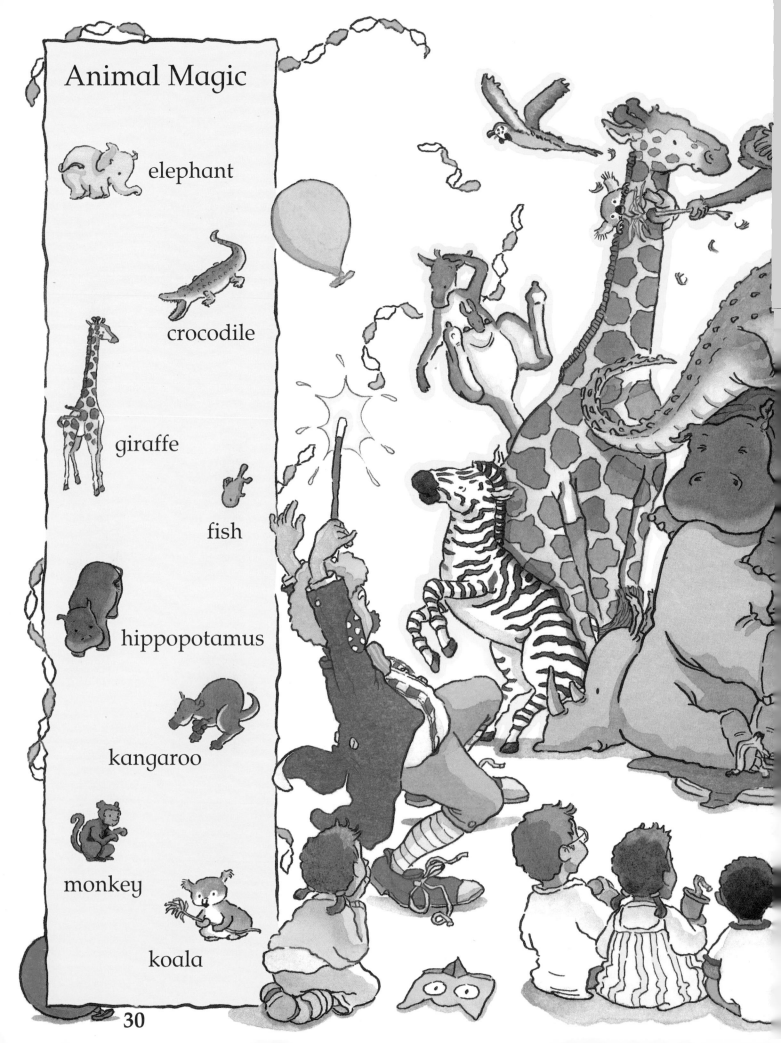

Animal Magic

elephant

crocodile

giraffe

fish

hippopotamus

kangaroo

monkey

koala

30

mouse

walrus

parrot

penguin

tiger

zebra

panda

rhinoceros

In the Bath

 dress

 jacket

 jumper

 shorts

 pants

 shirt

 shoes

 skirt

 socks

trousers

T-shirt

32

basin

bath

flannel

mirror

shower

soap

sponge

toilet

toilet paper

toothbrush

toothpaste

towel

Time for Bed

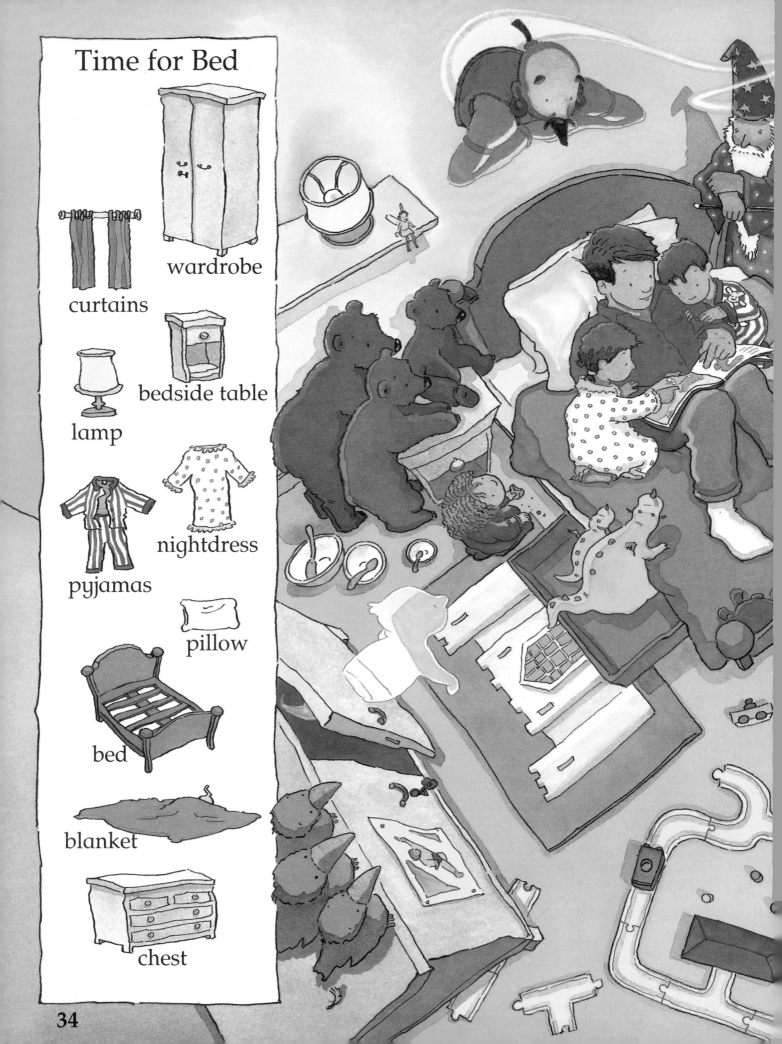

wardrobe

curtains

bedside table

lamp

nightdress

pyjamas

pillow

bed

blanket

chest

storybook

castle

king

queen

genie

magic lamp

dragon

giant

35

My ABC

A a   ant

B b   bell

C c   caterpillar

D d   dog

E e   egg

F f   fish

G g   goat

H h   helicopter

I i   ink

J j   juggler

K k   king

L l   ladybird

M m   mouse

N n   nail

O o   octopus

P p   puppet

Q q   queen

R r   ring

S s   socks

T t   tiger

U u   umbrella

V v   van

W w   watch

X x   X-ray

Y y   yacht

Z z   zebra

Count 123

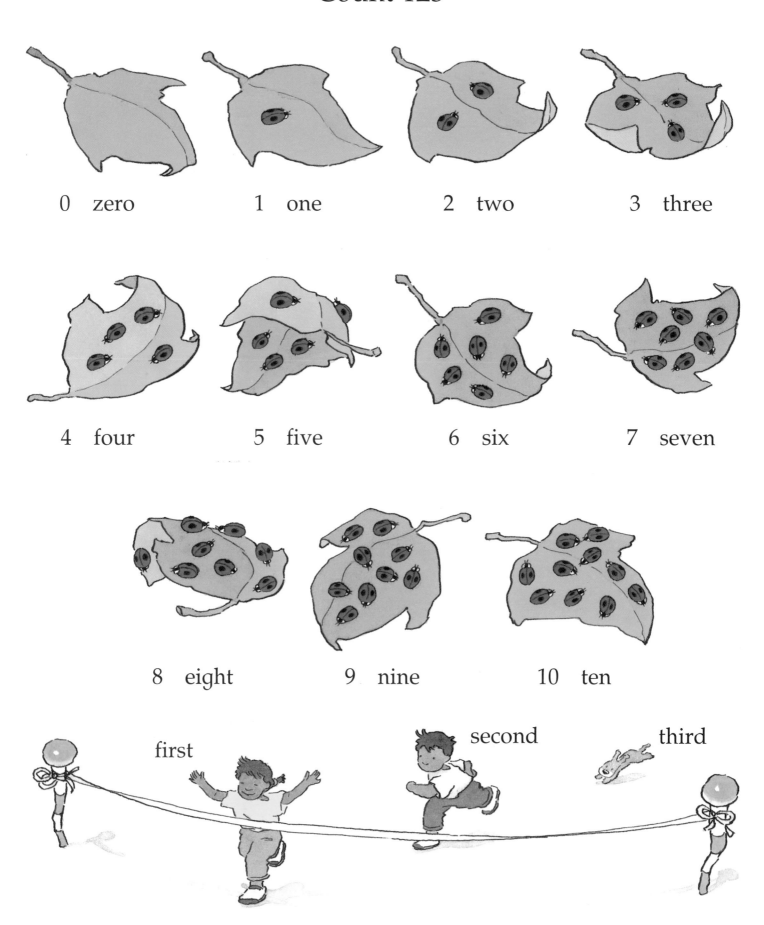

0 zero   1 one   2 two   3 three

4 four   5 five   6 six   7 seven

8 eight   9 nine   10 ten

first   second   third

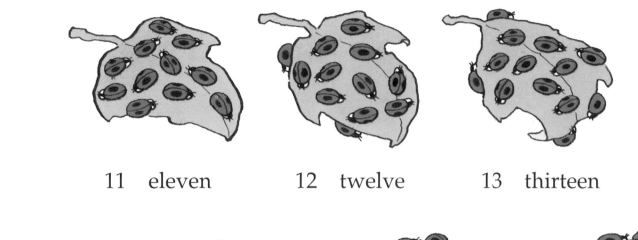

11   eleven   12   twelve   13   thirteen

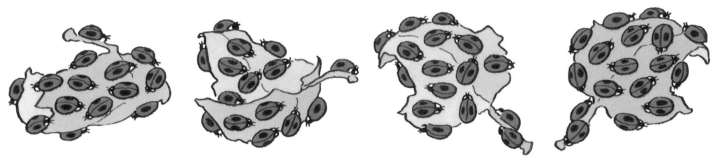

14   fourteen   15   fifteen   16   sixteen   17   seventeen

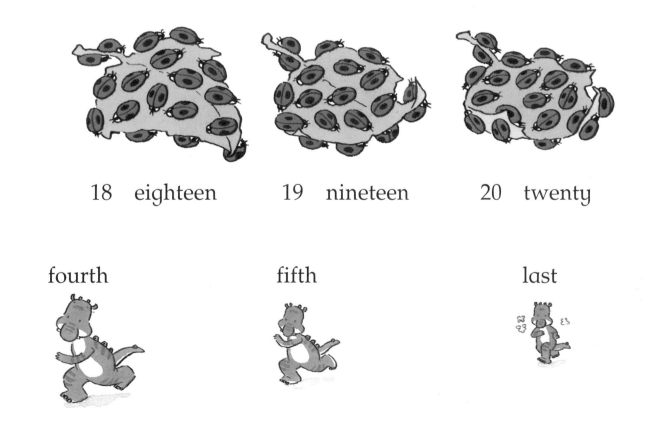

18   eighteen   19   nineteen   20   twenty

fourth   fifth   last

Shapes

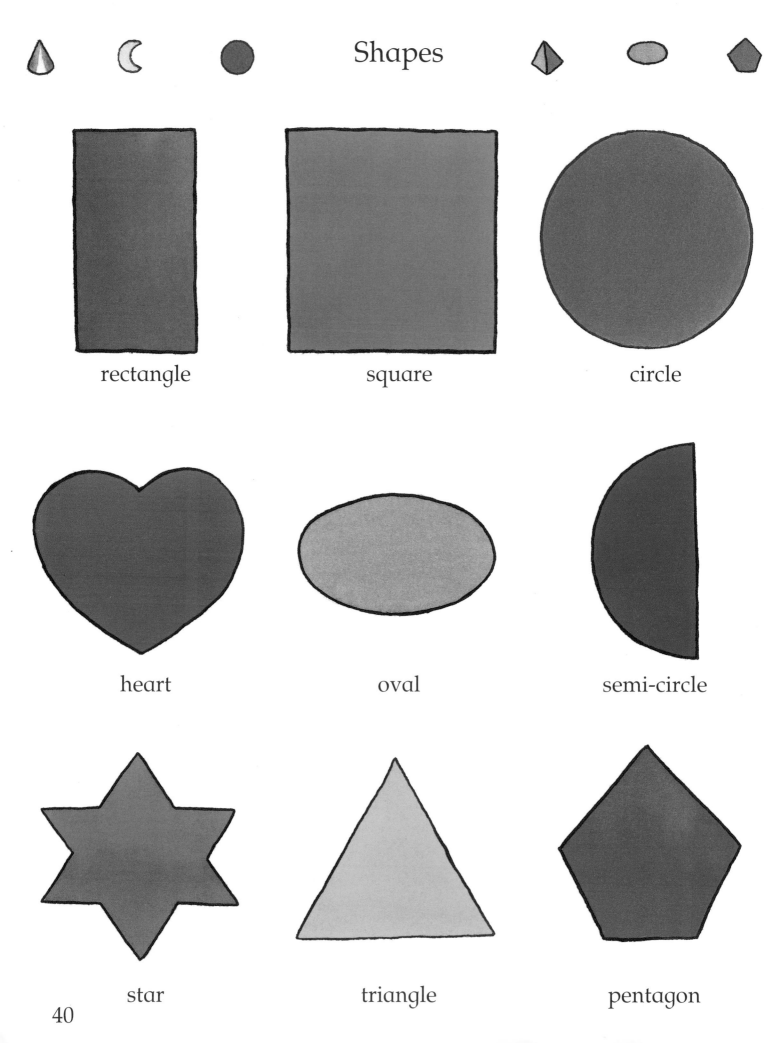

rectangle

square

circle

heart

oval

semi-circle

star

triangle

pentagon

40

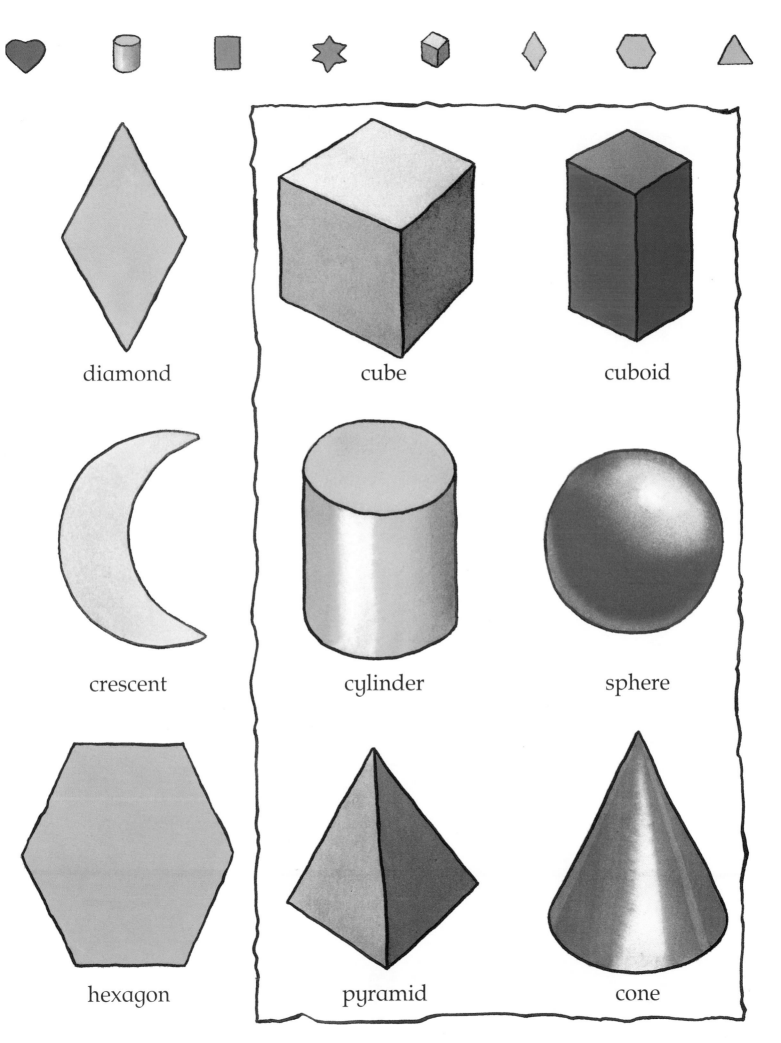

diamond

cube

cuboid

crescent

cylinder

sphere

hexagon

pyramid

cone

Opposites

big/small

clean/dirty

fat/thin

full/empty

high/low

hot/cold

new/old

open/closed

dark/light

fast/slow

happy/sad

heavy/light

long/short

more/less

same/different

wet/dry

43

cloudy

sunny

rainy

snowy

windy

foggy

eight o'clock

ten o'clock

twelve noon

two o'clock

four o'clock

six o'clock

Index

ambulance	9	cave painting	17	door	6	game	22
ant	36	cereal	18	dragon	35	garage	6
apple	19	chair	19	dress	32	gate	6
arm	4	chalk	10	drink	29	genie	35
astronaut	15	cheek	5	drum	23	giant	35
		cheese	19	dry	43	giraffe	30
back	4	chest (body)	4	duck	24	girl	5
ball	26	chest (furniture)	34	dustbin	6	globe	10
balloon	28	chicken	24			glue	13
banana	19	chimney	6			goat	24, 36
basin	33	chin	5	ear	5	goose	24
basket	18	chocolate	29	easel	13	green	12
bath	33	church	8	egg	36	grey	12
bed	34	circle	40	eggs	19	guitar	23
bedside table	34	clean	42	eight	38		
bell	36	closed	42	eighteen	39	hair	4
bells	23	cloudy	44	elbow	4	hand	4
bicycle	9	cock	24	elephant	30	happy	43
big	42	coins	17	eleven	39	hay	25
bin	10	cold	42	empty	42	head	4
birthday card	28	computer	11	eye	5	heart	40
biscuit	29	cone	41			heavy	43
black	12	cook	15	face	5	helicopter	9, 36
blackboard	10	cooker	20	fast	43	hexagon	41
blanket	34	cow	24	fat	42	high	42
blue	12	crab	27	felt pen	13	hill	25
bone	16	crescent	41	fence	6	hippopotamus	30
book	10	crocodile	30	field	25	horse	24
bottom	4	cube	41	fifteen	39	hot	42
bowl	20	cuboid	41	fifth	39		
boy	5	cup	20	finger	4	ice cream	29
bread	18	curtains	34	fire	17	ink	36
bridge	25	cushion	21	fire engine	9	iron	20
brown	12	cylinder	41	firefighter	14		
bucket	26	cymbals	23	first	38	jacket	32
builder	14			fish	30, 36	jam	18
bun	18	dancer	15	five	38	jigsaw puzzle	22
bus	9	dark	43	flannel	33	juggler	36
bus driver	14	deckchair	26	flint	17	jumper	32
		desk	10	flower	7		
cake	29	diamond	41	foggy	44	kangaroo	30
candle	28	dice	11	foot	4	kettle	20
car	9	different	43	footballer	14	keyboard (music)	23
carrot	19	Diplodocus	16	forest	25	keyboard (PC)	11
cash register	18	dirty	42	fork	20	king	35, 36
cassette	11	disk	11	fossil	16	knee	4
cassette recorder	11	diver	15	four	38	knife	20
castle	35	doctor	14	fourteen	39	koala	30
cat	7	dog	7, 36	fourth	39		
caterpillar	36	doll	22	fridge	20	ladybird	36
cave	17	doll's house	22	full	42	lamp	34

46

lamp post	8	penguin	31
last	39	pentagon	40
leaf	7	Pharoah	17
leg	4	pig	24
less	43	pillow	34
letters	7	pilot	15
lettuce	19	pink	12
lifeguard	15	pizza	29
light	43	plane	9
lighthouse	27	plate	20
long	43	playground	8
low	42	police officer	14
lunch box	10	pop star	15
		post bag	7
magic lamp	35	postman	14
magician	28	potatoes	18
magnet	10	pottery	17
map	11	present	28
microphone	23	puppet	37
milk	19	purple	12
mirror	33	pyjamas	34
monkey	30	pyramid (Egypt)	17
more	43	pyramid (shape)	41
motorbike	9		
mouse (animal)	31,36	queen	35, 37
mouse (PC)	11		
mouth	5	rabbit	7
		racing car	22
nail	37	rainy	44
neck	5	recorder	23
new	42	rectangle	40
nightdress	34	red	12
nine	38	rhinoceros	31
nineteen	39	ring	37
nose	5	robot	22
		roof	6
octopus	27, 37	ruler	11
old	42		
one	38	sad	43
open	42	same	43
orange (colour)	12	sandcastle	27
orange (fruit)	19	sandwich	29
oval	40	saucepan	20
overalls	13	saucer	21
		sausages	18
paintbrush	13	scarecrow	25
painting	13	school	8
paints	13	school bag	10
panda	31	scissors	13
pants	32	seagull	27
paper	13	seaweed	27
parrot	31	second	38
party blower	28	see-saw	26
party hat	28	semi-circle	40
pavement	8	seven	38
pencil	13	seventeen	39

sheep	24	thirteen	39
shell	27	three	38
ship	27	tiger	31, 37
shirt	32	time	45
shoes	32	toe	4
shop	8	toilet	33
short	43	toilet paper	33
shorts	32	tomato	19
shoulders	4	tongue	5
shower	33	toothbrush	33
six	38	toothpaste	33
sixteen	39	towel	33
skeleton	16	tractor	25
skirt	32	traffic lights	8
slide	26	train driver	15
slow	43	train set	22
small	42	tree	7
snail	7	triangle	40
snowy	44	Triceratops	16
soap	33	trolley	18
socks	32, 37	trousers	32
sofa	21	truck	9
soldier	17	trumpet	23
spade	26	tummy	4
spaghetti	18	twelve	39
sphere	41	twenty	39
sphinx	17	two	38
spider	7	Tyrannosaurus Rex	16
sponge	33		
spoon	21	umbrella	26, 37
square	40		
stairs	6	vacuum cleaner	21
star	40	van	37
starfish	27	vet	14
Stegosaurus	16	video recorder	21
stereo	21		
storybook	35	walrus	31
straw	29	wand	28
stream	25	wardrobe	34
streamer	28	washing machine	20
street	8	watch	37
suncream	26	wet	43
sunny	44	white	12
sweets	29	window	6
swing	26	windy	44
T-shirt	32	X-ray	37
table	21		
tambourine	23		
teapot	21	yacht	37
teddy	22	yellow	12
teeth	5	yoghurt	19
television	21		
ten	38	zebra	31, 37
thin	42	zebra crossing	8
third	38	zero	38

47